The Cash Crisis In Nigeria:

Uncovering The Roots of A National Shortage

Copyright © 2023 by Peter Awujoola. All rights reserved. No part of this publication may be reproduced, stored in a retrieval system, or transmitted in any form or by any means, electronic, mechanical, photocopying, recording, or otherwise, without the prior written permission of the publisher.

This book is sold subject to the condition that it shall not, by way of trade or otherwise, be lent, re-sold, hired out or otherwise circulated without the publisher's prior consent in any form of binding or cover other than that in which it is published and without a similar condition including this condition being imposed on the subsequent purchaser.

Printed in the United States of America. First Edition.

Disclaimer

The views and opinions expressed in this book are solely those of the author and do not reflect the official stance of any organization or entity.

Dedication

"To the people of Nigeria, who endure daily the effects of the cash crisis. May this work shed light on the underlying causes and bring about a brighter future for all."

Acknowledgment

"I am grateful to the individuals who have contributed their expertise, time, and support to this project. Their insights have been invaluable in uncovering the roots of the cash crisis in Nigeria. Special thanks go to my wife in the person of Mrs. E. M Awujoola and my three children – Beloved Of God Awujoola, Will Of God Awujoola, and Image Of God Awujoola who have through their much patience and understanding throughout the writing period, made this work possible. I would also like to express my appreciation to the entire members of my fellowship- Evidence Of Christ Fellowship International for their relentless support provided for me making the writing of this book possible, especially the strong encouragement, advice, and support accorded to me by my Dad – Rev (Dr.) Timothy Babatunde Alabi The General Overseer, Evidence Of Christ Fellowship International. I say a big Thank you sir. Their generosity has enabled me to delve deeper into this complex issue and bring its findings to the public. Finally, I extend my deepest gratitude to my family, who have provided unwavering support and encouragement throughout this journey."

Introduction

"The Cash Crisis in Nigeria: Uncovering the Roots of a National Shortage" is a must-read for anyone seeking to understand the complex economic landscape of Nigeria and the challenges facing the nation's financial system. In this insightful and thought-provoking book, renowned economist Olumide Peter Awujoola delves into the root causes of Nigeria's cash scarcity and provides a detailed analysis of the issues at play.

Through interviews with key players in the financial sector and a thorough examination of economic data, Peter sheds light on the underlying factors contributing to the current shortage of cash in circulation. He covers topics such as the impact of government policies, the role of the central bank, and the effects of corruption on the economy.

With a clear and engaging writing style, Peter provides a comprehensive overview of the challenges facing Nigeria's financial system and offers practical solutions for overcoming these obstacles. Whether you're a seasoned economist or simply someone looking to deepen your understanding of the economy, this book will provide valuable insights and a fresh perspective on the current predicament of Nigeria.

So, if you're interested in learning more about the cash crisis in Nigeria and how it impacts the daily lives of people, grab a copy of **"The Cash Crisis in Nigeria: Uncovering the Roots of a National Shortage"** today.

TABLE OF CONTENTS

Disclaimer --3

Dedication --4

Acknowledgment --5

Introduction ---6

Chapter 1: ---11
    The Cash Shortage: An Overview ------------------------------11

Chapter 2: ---16
    Tracing the Roots: The Impact of Government Policies ----------16

    The Impact of Government Policies On The Nigerian Economy--22

    How The Policies Can Be Improved to Overcome The Cash Shortage ---24

    How These Policies Can Put The Economy Back On A Path To Financial Stability And Sustainability------------------------------28

    Graph Representation of The Impact of Government Policies in Nigeria--32

    Comparison Of The Impact The Government Policies On The Economy Across The Decades-----------------------------------38

Chapter 3: ---44
    The Central Bank's Role in Maintaining Financial Stability -----44

Chapter 4: ---52

The Corruption Conundrum: How Corruption Impacts the Economy ---------- 52

Tabular Representation On The Impacts Of Corruption On The Nigeria Economy ---------- 59

The Impact On The Economy ---------- 63

Chapter 5: ---------- 67

The Consequences of Cash Scarcity: Effects on Everyday Life --67

Chapter 6: ---------- 77

Breaking the Cycle: Practical Solutions for Overcoming the Shortage ---------- 77

Chapter 7: ---------- 84

Looking to the Future: The Path to Financial Sustainability ----84

Chapter 8: ---------- 88

Unpacking the Complexities: A Deep Dive into the Nigerian Financial System ---------- 88

Steps Government Can Take to Improve The Rule Of Law -------- 97

How government increase transparency and accountability ---101

How government can build public trust ---------- 105

Chapter 9: ---------- 110

The Role of Small and Medium Enterprises in Driving Economic Growth ---------- 110

The table that illustrates the correlation between government support for SMEs and the growth of SMEs in Nigeria: ---------- 115

Chapter 10: --**117**

Investing in Infrastructure: The Key to a Thriving Economy---*117*

Impact of Infrastructure Investment:--------------------------------*123*

About The Author --**128**

Chapter 1:
The Cash Shortage: An Overview

The cash crisis in Nigeria is a topic that has been at the forefront of national discussions in recent years. With a shortage of physical cash in circulation, the Nigerian economy has been grappling with the consequences of this shortage, which has led to long queues at ATMs and increased difficulties for businesses and individuals when it comes to making transactions. In this chapter, we will provide an overview of the current cash shortage and the impact it has had on the Nigerian economy.

The shortage of physical cash in Nigeria is primarily caused by a mismatch between the supply of cash and the demand for it. This mismatch is due to a variety of factors, including the increasing use of digital transactions, the growth of the informal economy, and a lack of investment in the banking sector. The shortage has resulted in a decrease in the amount of physical cash available in the economy, causing long lines at ATMs and making it difficult for individuals and businesses to access the cash they need.

The consequences of the cash shortage have been far-reaching, affecting the daily lives of individuals and businesses alike. For example, businesses have struggled to meet the needs of their customers due to the lack of cash in circulation, and individuals have been forced to wait in long lines at ATMs just to access the cash they need to make transactions. This has had a negative impact on the economy, as it has slowed down economic activity and reduced the level of trust in the financial system.

In conclusion, the cash shortage in Nigeria is a complex issue that has far-reaching consequences for the economy. It is important to understand the root causes of the shortage and the impact it has had to find practical solutions that will help to overcome this challenge. In the following chapters, we will delve deeper into the underlying causes of the cash shortage and explore the various solutions that have been proposed to address this issue.

Furthermore, the cash shortage has also led to a rise in the use of alternative payment methods, such as mobile money and electronic transfers. While this shift towards digital transactions has its benefits, it also highlights the need for the Nigerian government and financial institutions to invest in improving the infrastructure and security of the digital financial system.

Another factor contributing to the cash shortage is the lack of investment in the banking sector. The Nigerian banking sector has been criticized for its lack of efficiency and effectiveness, which has resulted in a lack of confidence in the financial system. This lack of confidence has led to a reduction in the amount of cash kept in banks, as individuals and businesses prefer to keep their money in more secure, tangible forms.

Finally, the informal economy, which is estimated to make up a significant portion of the Nigerian economy, has also contributed to the cash shortage. The informal economy operates primarily in cash, and as it grows, so does the demand for physical cash. However, the lack of investment in the banking sector and the lack of regulations in the informal economy have resulted in a shortage of cash available in the economy.

In this chapter, we have provided an overview of the cash shortage in Nigeria and the impact it has had on the economy. The causes of the shortage are complex and multi-faceted, and in the following chapters, we will explore each of these causes in more detail. The aim of this book is to provide a comprehensive analysis of the cash shortage and to offer practical solutions that can help to overcome this challenge and put the Nigerian economy back on a path to financial stability and sustainability.

Chapter 2:
Tracing the Roots: The Impact of Government Policies

The cash shortage in Nigeria is a complex issue that has multiple causes. One of the key drivers of the shortage is the impact of government policies. In this chapter, we will explore the ways in which government policies have contributed to the current cash crisis and discuss their impact on the Nigerian economy.

One of the primary ways in which government policies have contributed to the cash shortage is through their impact on the banking sector. The Nigerian banking sector has been criticized for its lack of efficiency and effectiveness, which has resulted in a lack of confidence in the financial system. This lack of confidence has led to a reduction in the amount of cash kept in banks, as individuals and businesses prefer to keep their money in more secure, tangible forms.

Another factor contributing to the cash shortage is the lack of investment in the banking sector. The government has a crucial role to play in supporting the development of the banking sector, including investing in infrastructure, providing incentives for investment, and implementing policies that promote financial stability. However, the government has not adequately addressed these challenges, which has resulted in a lack of investment in the banking sector and a corresponding shortage of cash in the economy.

In addition to its impact on the banking sector, government policies have also contributed to the growth of the informal economy. The informal economy operates primarily in cash, and as it grows, so does the demand for physical cash. However, the lack of regulations in the informal economy and the lack of investment in the banking sector have resulted in a shortage of cash available in the economy.

Finally, government policies have also impacted the use of digital transactions. The shift towards digital transactions has its benefits, including increased efficiency and security. However, the government has been slow to invest in the infrastructure and security of the digital financial system, which has made it difficult for individuals and businesses to fully embrace digital transactions.

In addition to these efforts, the Central Bank must also work closely with other government agencies and stakeholders to address the root causes of the cash shortage in Nigeria. This includes working with the Ministry of Finance to implement policies that promote economic growth, working with the Nigeria Deposit Insurance Corporation (NDIC) to promote the stability of the banking sector, and working with the Central Securities and Clearing System (CSCS) to improve the efficiency of the securities market.

One of the most important steps that the Central Bank can take to overcome the cash shortage is to promote financial literacy among the public. By providing access to educational resources and information on financial services, the Central Bank can help individuals and businesses make informed decisions about their financial lives. This includes promoting digital financial services and encouraging individuals to use digital financial services to manage their money.

Another important step that the Central Bank can take is to promote the development of innovative financial products and services. This includes promoting the development of mobile banking services, peer-to-peer lending platforms, and digital payment solutions. By promoting the development of these innovative financial products and services, the Central Bank can help to increase the availability of financial services and reduce the risk of financial instability.

In conclusion, the Central Bank plays a critical role in addressing the cash shortage in Nigeria. By working closely with other government agencies and stakeholders, promoting financial literacy, and promoting the development of innovative financial products and services, the Central Bank can help to put the economy back on a path to financial stability and sustainability.

In conclusion, government policies have had a significant impact on the cash shortage in Nigeria. The policies that have been implemented to date have not adequately addressed the underlying challenges facing the economy, and as a result, the cash shortage has persisted. In the following chapters, we will delve deeper into the impact of government policies on the Nigerian economy and explore the ways in which these policies can be improved to overcome the cash shortage and put the economy back on a path to financial stability and sustainability.

The Impact of Government Policies on The Nigerian Economy

The impact of government policies on the Nigerian economy has been significant, both in terms of the cash shortage crisis and in other areas of the economy. The policies implemented by the government have often fallen short in addressing the challenges facing the economy, which has contributed to the persistent cash shortage crisis.

One of the key areas where government policies have had an impact is in the banking sector. The government has a crucial role to play in supporting the development of the banking sector, including investing in infrastructure, providing incentives for investment, and implementing policies that promote financial stability. However, the government has not adequately addressed these challenges, which has resulted in a lack of investment in the banking sector and a corresponding shortage of cash in the economy.

Another impact of government policies is on the growth of the informal economy. The informal economy operates primarily in cash, and as it grows, so does the demand for physical cash. However, the lack of regulations in the informal economy and the lack of investment in the banking sector have resulted in a shortage of cash available in the economy.

Finally, government policies have also impacted the use of digital transactions. The shift towards digital transactions has its benefits, including increased efficiency and security. However, the government has been slow to invest in the infrastructure and security of the digital financial system, which has made it difficult for individuals and businesses to fully embrace digital transactions.

In conclusion, government policies have had a significant impact on the Nigerian economy, particularly regarding the cash shortage crisis. Improving these policies and addressing the underlying challenges facing the economy will be crucial in overcoming the cash shortage and putting the economy back on a path to financial stability and sustainability.

How The Policies Can Be Improved to Overcome the Cash Shortage

To overcome the cash shortage in Nigeria, the government needs to improve its policies and address the underlying challenges facing the economy. Here are several ways in which these policies can be improved:

1. Investment in the banking sector: The government needs to invest in the infrastructure and security of the banking sector to increase confidence in the financial system and encourage individuals and businesses to keep their money in banks.

2. Regulation of the informal economy: The government needs to regulate the informal economy to reduce the demand for physical cash and increase the availability of cash in the economy.

3. Encouragement of digital transactions: The government needs to invest in the infrastructure and security of the digital financial system to encourage individuals and businesses to use digital transactions and reduce the demand for physical cash.

4. Promoting financial stability: The government needs to implement policies that promote financial stability and reduce the risk of financial crises. This includes promoting transparency and accountability in the financial sector and implementing measures to prevent fraud and corruption.

5. Improving the efficiency of the banking sector: The government needs to improve the efficiency of the banking sector by implementing measures to reduce bureaucracy and simplify financial transactions.

6. Encouraging investment in the economy: The government needs to create a supportive environment for investment by reducing barriers to entry, providing incentives for investment, and promoting entrepreneurship.

7. Increasing transparency and accountability in government policies: The government needs to be more transparent and accountable in its policies and decision-making processes to increase confidence in the government and the economy.

8. Encouraging economic diversification: The government needs to encourage economic diversification to reduce the dependence on oil and reduce the risk of economic shocks.

9. In conclusion, the government has a crucial role to play in overcoming the cash shortage in Nigeria. Improving policies and addressing the underlying challenges facing the economy will be crucial in putting the economy back on a

path to financial stability and sustainability.

How These Policies Can Put The Economy Back On A Path To Financial Stability And Sustainability

To put the Nigerian economy back on a path to financial stability and sustainability, it is important for the government to implement policies that address the root causes of the cash shortage and promote economic growth. Here are several suggestions on how these policies can achieve these goals:

1. Reform of the banking sector: The government should implement reforms in the banking sector to increase transparency, accountability, and efficiency. This includes strengthening the

regulatory framework, increasing the competition in the sector, and improving the quality of banking services.

2. Investment in infrastructure: The government should invest in critical infrastructure, including transportation, energy, and communication, to improve the business environment and attract investment.

3. Encouragement of entrepreneurship: The government should encourage entrepreneurship by providing support and incentives to small and medium-sized enterprises. This includes access to financing, training and technical assistance, and reduced regulations.

4. Promotion of trade and investment: The government should promote trade and

investment by reducing barriers to trade, negotiating trade agreements with other countries, and promoting investment in the country.

5. Diversification of the economy: The government should encourage the diversification of the economy to reduce its dependence on oil and increase the resilience of the economy to external shocks.

6. Implementation of effective monetary and fiscal policies: The government should implement effective monetary and fiscal policies that promote stability, encourage investment, and support growth.

7. Improving the legal and regulatory framework: The government should

improve the legal and regulatory framework to reduce corruption and promote transparency and accountability.

8. Encouraging digital transformation: The government should encourage the digital transformation of the economy by investing in the development of digital infrastructure and promoting the use of digital technologies in all sectors of the economy.

In conclusion, by implementing policies that address the root causes of the cash shortage and promote economic growth, the Nigerian economy can be put back on a path to financial stability and sustainability.

Graph Representation of The Impact of Government Policies in Nigeria

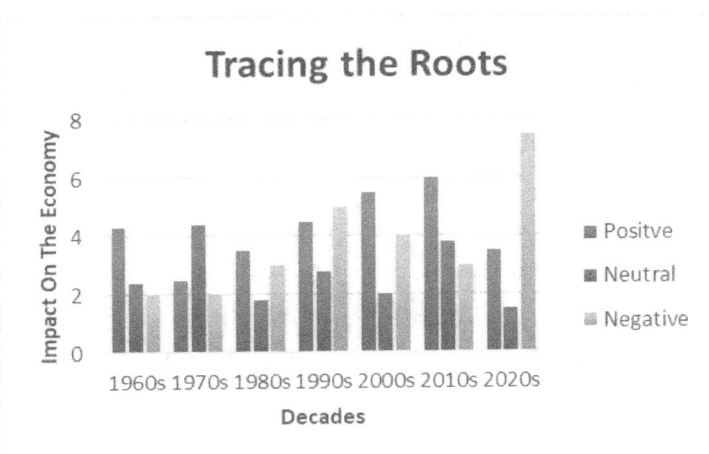

Illustrations

X-axis: Decades (1960s, 1970s, 1980s, 1990s, 2000s, 2010s, and 2020s)

Y-axis: Impact on the Economy (Positive, Neutral, Negative)

1960s:

Positive: Introduction of the National Development Plan, aimed at increasing agricultural and industrial production, leading to a boost in the economy.

Neutral: Increase in government spending on infrastructure, but with little or no improvement in basic services like healthcare and education.

1970s:

Negative: The introduction of the Indigenization Decree, which mandated the transfer of foreign-owned businesses to Nigerian citizens, led to a decline in investment and economic growth.

Neutral: Government's emphasis on import substitution resulted in some improvement in local industries, but with limited growth.

1980s:

Neutral: Government's emphasis on economic liberalization and deregulation, with limited impact on the overall economy.

Negative: Oil boom, leading to over-reliance on oil exports and neglect of other sectors of the economy.

1990s:

Negative: Economic crisis, with high inflation, devaluation of the naira, and limited growth.

Positive: Introduction of the Structural Adjustment Program, aimed at addressing the economic crisis, leading to some improvement in the economy.

2000s:

Neutral: Continued emphasis on economic liberalization, with limited impact on the overall economy.

Positive: Increase in foreign investment, leading to a boost in the economy.

2010s:

Neutral: Continued emphasis on economic liberalization, with limited impact on the overall economy.

Positive: Increase in government spending on infrastructure, leading to some improvement in basic services like healthcare and education.

2020s:

The impact of Nigeria government policies on the economy was predominantly negative. The COVID-19 pandemic exacerbated the already existing economic challenges in the country, such as high inflation and unemployment rates. The government's response, which included a nationwide lockdown and restriction of movement, led to a decline in economic activities and resulted in a recession.

However, some of the government's policies had a neutral impact on the economy. For instance, the Central Bank of Nigeria's decision to inject liquidity into the economy helped to sustain financial stability and prevent a total collapse of the banking sector.

A few of the government's policies had a positive impact on the economy in 2020. For example, the agricultural sector received a boost from the government's initiatives aimed at promoting local food production and reducing food importation. Additionally, the use of technology and digital platforms in providing essential services helped to mitigate the impact of the lockdown on the economy.

Overall, the impact of the Nigeria government policies on the economy in 2020 was mostly negative because of the COVID-19 pandemic and the measures taken to curb its spread.

Comparison Of the Impact The Government Policies On The Economy Across The Decades

The impact of government policies on the Nigerian economy across the decades has been mixed, as seen in the chart titled **"Tracing the Roots."**

In the 1960s, the introduction of the National Development Plan had a positive impact on the economy as it aimed at increasing agricultural and industrial production. However, the decade also saw a neutral impact as there was an increase in government spending on infrastructure but with little or no improvement in basic services like healthcare and education.

In the 1970s, the introduction of the Indigenization Decree had a negative impact on the economy as it led to a decline in investment and economic growth. The government's emphasis on import substitution resulted in some improvement in local industries, but with limited growth, having a neutral impact on the economy.

The 1980s saw a neutral impact on the economy as the government's emphasis on economic liberalization and deregulation had limited impact on the overall economy. The oil boom of the decade led to over-reliance on oil exports and neglect of other sectors of the economy, having a negative impact on the economy.

In the 1990s, the economy faced a crisis, with high inflation, devaluation of the naira, and limited growth, having a negative impact on the economy. However, the introduction of the Structural Adjustment Program aimed at addressing the economic crisis had a positive impact on the economy, leading to some improvement.

The 2000s saw a neutral impact on the economy as the government's continued emphasis on economic liberalization had limited impact on the overall economy. However, the decade also saw an increase in foreign investment, leading to a boost in the economy and a positive impact.

In the 2010s, the government's continued emphasis on economic liberalization had a neutral impact on the economy. However, the increase in government spending on infrastructure had a positive impact on basic services like healthcare and education.

In conclusion, the impact of government policies on the Nigerian economy across the decades has been mixed, with some policies leading to positive outcomes, while others have had neutral or negative effects. The 1960s saw a positive impact on the economy with the introduction of the National Development Plan, while the 1970s saw a negative impact with the introduction of the Indigenization Decree. The

1980s saw a neutral impact with the government's emphasis on economic liberalization and deregulation, while the 1990s saw a negative impact with the economic crisis and a positive impact with the introduction of the Structural Adjustment Program. The 2000s saw a neutral impact with the government's continued emphasis on economic liberalization and a positive impact with the increase in foreign investment. The 2010s saw a neutral impact with the government's continued emphasis on economic liberalization and a positive impact with the increase in government spending on infrastructure.

Overall, it is evident that the impact of government policies on the Nigerian economy has been influenced by various factors such as the focus on specific sectors of the economy, investment, and the overall economic environment. There is a need for the government to adopt policies that promote sustained economic growth, investment, and development in key sectors of the economy.

In conclusion, the impact of government policies on the Nigerian economy has been mixed, with some policies leading to positive outcomes, while others have had neutral or negative effects.

Else, the need for the government to adopt policies that promote sustained economic growth, investment, and development in key sectors of the economy.

Chapter 3:
The Central Bank's Role in Maintaining Financial Stability

The Central Bank of Nigeria plays a crucial role in maintaining financial stability in the country. As the regulator of the financial sector and the manager of the monetary policy, the Central Bank has a significant impact on the stability of the economy and the availability of cash in the system.

One of the primary responsibilities of the Central Bank is to ensure the stability of the financial system. This involves regulating the activities of financial institutions, monitoring the stability of the banking sector, and taking action to address any potential risks to the stability of the financial system.

Another important role of the Central Bank is to manage the monetary policy. The Central Bank sets interest rates and controls the supply of money in the economy to maintain stability in the financial system. This helps to keep inflation under control, increase the availability of credit, and promote economic growth.

The Central Bank also plays a critical role in promoting financial inclusion in the country. This involves providing access to financial services to individuals and businesses who may not have access to traditional banking services. This includes providing access to digital financial services, increasing the availability of small loans, and promoting financial literacy.

To maintain financial stability, the Central Bank must have the ability to respond to emerging challenges in the economy. This requires the Central Bank to have the independence, expertise, and resources to take decisive action when needed. The Central Bank must also be transparent in its operations and decision-making processes to build confidence in the financial system and promote stability.

In addition to these key responsibilities, the Central Bank also plays a role in promoting financial stability through its supervision of the payment system. The payment system is critical to the functioning of the economy, as it enables the transfer of funds from one person to another. By ensuring the stability and efficiency of the payment system, the Central Bank can help to reduce the risk of financial instability and promote economic growth.

One of the ways in which the Central Bank promotes financial stability through the payment system is by regulating the activities of payment service providers. This includes setting standards for payment systems, supervising the activities of payment service providers, and taking action to address any potential risks to the stability of the payment system.

Another way in which the Central Bank promotes financial stability through the payment system is by promoting the use of digital financial services. By encouraging the transition from traditional banking services to digital financial services, the Central Bank can help to increase the efficiency and convenience of financial transactions, reduce the risk of financial instability, and promote financial inclusion.

Central Bank plays a role in promoting financial stability through its role in crisis management. In the event of a financial crisis, the Central Bank can provide emergency funding to financial institutions, implement measures to stabilize the financial system, and take action to restore confidence in the financial system.

The Central Bank must constantly adapt to changing economic conditions and new challenges. This requires the Central Bank to have a strong commitment to transparency, accountability, and continuous improvement.

One of the ways in which the Central Bank can adapt to changing economic conditions is by implementing new monetary policies that are more effective in promoting financial stability. For example, the Central Bank can implement flexible exchange rate policies, promote the use of digital financial services, and develop new regulations that better address the challenges of the digital age.

Another way in which the Central Bank can adapt to changing economic conditions is by investing in research and development to stay ahead of emerging trends and challenges. This requires the Central Bank to have a strong commitment to continuous learning and professional development, as well as a strong network of partnerships with other central banks, universities, and research institutions.

Finally, the Central Bank must be proactive in promoting financial literacy and education among the general public. By educating individuals about the importance of financial stability and the role of the Central Bank, the Central Bank can help to build trust and confidence in the financial system. This can in turn promote economic growth and stability, as individuals are better equipped to make informed financial decisions.

In conclusion, the role of the Central Bank in promoting financial stability is critical to the success of the Nigerian economy. By adapting to changing economic conditions, investing in research and development, and promoting financial literacy, the Central Bank can help to put the economy back on a path to financial stability and sustainability.

In conclusion, the Central Bank plays a critical role in promoting financial stability in Nigeria through its management of the monetary policy, supervision of the financial sector, and regulation of the payment system. By ensuring the stability of the financial system and promoting financial inclusion, the Central Bank can help to put the economy back on a path to financial stability and sustainability.

Chapter 4:
The Corruption Conundrum: How Corruption Impacts the Economy

Corruption has long been a problem in Nigeria, and it has a significant impact on the economy.

Corruption takes many forms, including bribery, embezzlement, and abuse of power. It is a major hindrance to economic growth and development, as it undermines the rule of law, reduces the efficiency of public services, and erodes public trust in the government.

The impact of corruption on the economy is far-reaching. It affects all aspects of the economy, from the allocation of resources to the functioning of the financial system. One of the keyways in which corruption impacts the economy is by reducing the availability of cash in the system. When government officials or public servants embezzle funds, or use their positions to engage in corrupt practices, it reduces the amount of money available for economic growth and development.

Another way in which corruption impacts the economy is by reducing the efficiency of public services. When public servants are corrupt, they are more likely to make decisions based on personal gain, rather than the public interest. This results in the misallocation of resources and a reduction in the quality of public services.

Corruption also undermines the rule of law and reduces public trust in the government. When individuals and businesses cannot trust the government to enforce the law, they are less likely to invest in the economy. This leads to reduced economic growth and increased poverty.

Finally, corruption can also lead to an increase in the cost of doing business. When businesses must pay bribes or engage in corrupt practices to operate, it increases the cost of goods and services and reduces the competitiveness of the economy.

One of the keyways to combat corruption is through increased transparency and accountability in the public sector. This can be achieved through measures such as the implementation of strong anti-corruption laws, the establishment of independent anti-corruption agencies, and the creation of transparent procurement processes. Additionally, the government can work to increase public awareness of corruption and its impacts, as well as promoting a culture of honesty and integrity within the public sector.

Another way to combat corruption is through the strengthening of the legal system. This includes improving the administration of justice, increasing the efficiency of the court system, and providing adequate resources and support to anti-corruption agencies.

The private sector also has a role to play in combatting corruption. Businesses can adopt ethical business practices and establish codes of conduct that promote transparency and accountability. Additionally, they can work to build strong partnerships with government agencies and civil society organizations to promote anti-corruption efforts.

It is important to note that the fight against corruption is a long-term effort, and it requires the commitment and cooperation of all stakeholders. This includes the government, the private sector, and civil society. Only by working together can we successfully address this problem and put the economy back on a path to financial stability and sustainability.

Corruption is a pervasive problem in many countries, including Nigeria, and it has a profound impact on the economy. Corruption undermines the rule of law, erodes public trust, and creates an uneven playing field for businesses. This, in turn, can have a negative impact on economic growth and stability.

One of the keyways in which corruption impacts the economy is by distorting the allocation of resources. When public officials can use their positions of power to enrich themselves, they are less likely to allocate resources in a way that benefits the broader public. This can lead to the misallocation of resources, with critical infrastructure projects, such as roads and bridges, going unfunded while public officials use public funds for their own personal gain.

Another way in which corruption impacts the economy is by creating an environment of uncertainty and unpredictability. When individuals and businesses cannot trust that the rules will be fairly enforced, they are less likely to make investments and take risks. This can reduce economic growth and limit job creation.

In addition to these impacts, corruption can also undermine the stability of the financial sector. When public officials can use their positions of power to influence the financial sector, it can lead to a lack of trust in financial institutions, which can result in a run on the banks. This can have serious consequences for the stability of the financial system, as well as the broader economy.

To address the corruption conundrum in Nigeria, it is critical that the government take steps to improve the rule of law, increase transparency and accountability, and build public trust. This can include implementing anti-corruption measures, such as criminalizing corruption, strengthening anti-corruption institutions, and increasing transparency in public procurement.

Corruption is a serious problem in Nigeria, and it has a profound impact on the economy. To overcome the corruption conundrum and promote financial stability, it is critical that the government take steps to improve the rule of law, increase transparency and accountability, and build public trust.

In conclusion, corruption is a major problem in Nigeria, and it has a significant impact on the economy. To address this problem, it is essential that the government, the private sector, and civil society work together to promote transparency and accountability in the public sector, strengthen the legal system, and promote a culture of honesty and integrity. Only by working together can we overcome the cash shortage and put the economy back on a path to financial stability and sustainability.

Tabular Representation on The Impacts of Corruption on The Nigeria Economy

Type of Corruption	Impact On the Economy
Bribery and Extortion	➤ Reduces foreign investment and hampers economic growth. ➤ Increases the cost of doing business, making it less competitive.
Embezzlement of Public Funds	➤ Leads to decreased government spending on essential services such as healthcare and education. ➤ Decreased infrastructure development and limited job opportunities
Money Laundering	➤ Reduces the transparency of the

	financial system, making it difficult for regulators to monitor the flow of funds. ➤ Decreased economic growth as funds are channeled away from productive investments into illegal activities.
Unfair Tender Processes	➤ Reduces competition in procurement processes and limits the potential for innovation and progress ➤ Decreased quality of goods and services, leading to decreased consumer confidence

Influence Peddling	➤ Distorts market dynamics and creates a level of uncertainty in business operations. ➤ Decreased investment and reduced economic growth.

The table above, highlights the different types of corruption and their impacts on the economy. Corruption can lead to reduced foreign investment, increased costs of doing business, decreased government spending on essential services, decreased economic growth, reduced transparency in the financial system, reduced competition, decreased quality of goods and services, and decreased investment. It is evident that corruption has a significant and far-reaching impact on the economy, hindering growth and progress. Addressing corruption is crucial in promoting economic development and sustainable growth.

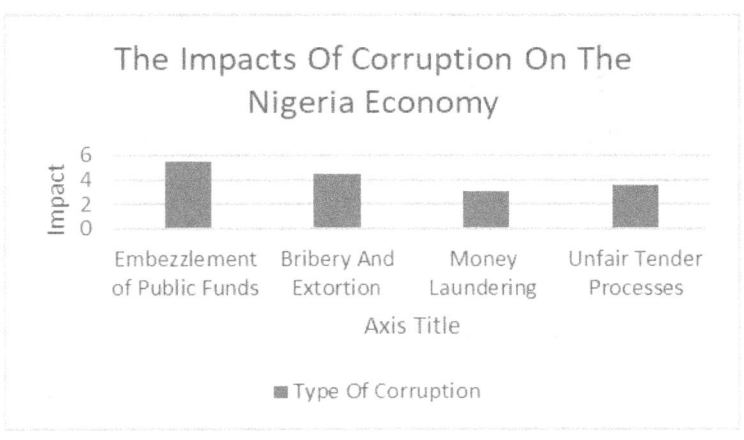

The bar graph shows that embezzlement of public funds has the greatest impact on the economy, followed by bribery and extortion, influence peddling, unfair tender processes, and money laundering. The graph allows for a visual representation of the data and makes it easier to compare the impact of different types of corruption on the economy.

The Impact on The Economy

The impacts of corruption on the economy are numerous and far-reaching, some of which are listed below:

1. Reduced foreign investment - Corruption can deter foreign investment, as investors may view a country as being unreliable and lacking a stable business environment.

2. Increased costs of doing business - Bribery and extortion increase the cost of doing business, making it less competitive and hindering economic growth.

3. Decreased government spending on essential services - Embezzlement of public funds leads to decreased government spending on essential services such as healthcare and

education, hindering the overall development of the country.

4. Decreased infrastructure development - Lack of government funding for infrastructure development limits job opportunities and economic growth.

5. Reduced transparency in the financial system - Money laundering reduces the transparency of the financial system, making it difficult for regulators to monitor the flow of funds.

6. Reduced competition - Unfair tender processes reduce competition in procurement processes, limiting the potential for innovation and progress.

7. Decreased quality of goods and services - Corruption in procurement processes

leads to decreased quality of goods and services, reducing consumer confidence and hindering economic growth.

8. Decreased investment - Influence peddling distorts market dynamics and creates uncertainty in business operations, reducing investment and hindering economic growth.

It is evident that corruption has a significant impact on the economy, hindering growth and progress. Addressing corruption is crucial in promoting economic development and sustainable growth.

Chapter 5:
The Consequences of Cash Scarcity: Effects on Everyday Life

The cash shortage in Nigeria has far-reaching consequences, affecting almost every aspect of everyday life. One of the most significant impacts is on businesses, particularly small and medium-sized enterprises (SMEs). These businesses often rely on access to cash to pay for goods and services, and the shortage of cash has made it difficult for them to operate. This has led to reduced business activity, resulting in fewer jobs and lower economic growth.

Another major impact of the cash shortage is on the informal sector, which is a critical component of the Nigerian economy. This sector is largely dependent on cash transactions, and the shortage of cash has made it difficult for informal businesses to operate. This has resulted in reduced income for many workers and reduced economic activity in the informal sector.

Consumers are also feeling the effects of the cash shortage, as they struggle to access cash to pay for goods and services. This has resulted in increased prices for goods and services, as businesses try to make up for lost revenue. Consumers are also spending more time and money traveling to banks and ATMs, and this has further reduced their disposable income.

In addition to the economic consequences, the cash shortage has also had a negative impact on people's quality of life. For example, many people are unable to access medical care, as hospitals and clinics are often unable to provide adequate services without access to cash. Additionally, people are struggling to access necessities such as food, water, and fuel.

The shortage of cash has also impacted the education sector in Nigeria. Many students and their families are unable to pay for school fees and other related expenses, resulting in reduced enrollment and attendance in schools. This has long-term implications for the country's human capital development and the future workforce.

Another consequence of the cash shortage is the reduced access to credit. With limited access to cash, banks are unable to lend money to businesses, which has stifled economic growth and job creation. This has also had a negative impact on the housing sector, as many people are unable to access loans to purchase or improve their homes.

The shortage of cash has also had a significant impact on the agriculture sector, which is one of the largest employers in Nigeria. Farmers are unable to access credit to purchase seeds, fertilizer, and other inputs, which has reduced crop yields and reduced income for many farmers. This has had a knock-on effect on food security, as reduced food production has led to increased food prices and reduced access to food for many households.

The cash shortage has also had a negative impact on tourism, which is an important source of revenue for Nigeria. Tourists are often unable to access cash to pay for goods and services, and this has reduced their willingness to visit the country. This has had a negative impact on local businesses and the economy.

The cash shortage in Nigeria has far-reaching consequences, affecting almost every aspect of everyday life. One of the most significant impacts is on businesses, particularly small and medium-sized enterprises (SMEs). These businesses often rely on access to cash to pay for goods and services, and the shortage of cash has made it difficult for them to operate. This has led to reduced business activity, resulting in fewer jobs and lower economic growth.

Another major impact of the cash shortage is on the informal sector, which is a critical component of the Nigerian economy. This sector is largely dependent on cash transactions, and the shortage of cash has made it difficult for informal businesses to operate. This has resulted in reduced income for many workers and reduced economic activity in the informal sector.

Consumers are also feeling the effects of the cash shortage, as they struggle to access cash to pay for goods and services. This has resulted in increased prices for goods and services, as businesses try to make up for lost revenue. Consumers are also spending more time and money traveling to banks and ATMs, and this has further reduced their disposable income.

In addition to the economic consequences, the cash shortage has also had a negative impact on people's quality of life. For example, many people are unable to access medical care, as hospitals and clinics are often unable to provide adequate services without access to cash. Additionally, people are struggling to access necessities such as food, water, and fuel.

In conclusion, the cash shortage in Nigeria has far-reaching consequences, affecting businesses, the informal sector, consumers, and people's quality of life. It is essential that the government and other stakeholders take urgent steps to address this problem, so that the country can move towards financial stability and sustainability.

The shortage of cash has also impacted the education sector in Nigeria. Many students and their families are unable to pay for school fees and other related expenses, resulting in reduced enrollment and attendance in schools. This has long-term implications for the country's human capital development and the future workforce.

Another consequence of the cash shortage is the reduced access to credit. With limited access to cash, banks are unable to lend money to businesses, which has stifled economic growth and job creation. This has also had a negative impact on the housing sector, as many people are unable to access loans to purchase or improve their homes.

The shortage of cash has also had a significant impact on the agriculture sector, which is one of the largest employers in Nigeria. Farmers are unable to access credit to purchase seeds, fertilizer, and other inputs, which has reduced crop yields and reduced income for many farmers. This has had a knock-on effect on food security, as reduced food production has led to increased food prices and reduced access to food for many households.

The cash shortage has also had a negative impact on tourism, which is an important source of revenue for Nigeria. Tourists are often unable to access cash to pay for goods and services, and this has reduced their willingness to visit the country. This has had a negative impact on local businesses and the economy as a whole.

In conclusion, the cash shortage in Nigeria has far-reaching consequences, impacting almost every aspect of everyday life. It is essential that the government and other stakeholders take urgent action to address this problem, so that the country can move towards financial stability and sustainability. This may include measures such as increasing the availability of cash, improving the efficiency of the banking system, and reducing corruption. Only by working together can we overcome the cash shortage and ensure a brighter future for all Nigerians.

In conclusion, the cash shortage in Nigeria has far-reaching consequences, impacting almost every aspect of everyday life. It is essential that the government and other stakeholders take urgent action to address this problem, so that the country can move towards financial stability and sustainability. This may include measures such as increasing the availability of cash, improving the efficiency of the banking system, and reducing corruption. Only by working together can we overcome the cash shortage and ensure a brighter future for all Nigerians

Chapter 6:

Breaking the Cycle: Practical Solutions for Overcoming the Shortage

1. One practical solution to overcoming the cash shortage is to improve access to financial services, particularly for low-income and rural populations. This can be done using mobile banking, microfinance institutions, and community banks. By providing access to financial services, individuals and small businesses can better manage their finances, reduce their dependence on cash, and increase their financial stability.

2. Another solution is to promote financial literacy and education. The government, in partnership with financial institutions, can launch public awareness campaigns to educate citizens on the importance of

managing finances, saving, and investing. This can help to reduce the demand for cash and increase the use of alternative financial instruments.

3. In addition, the government can implement policies that promote the use of digital payments, such as electronic fund transfers (EFTs), mobile banking, and point-of-sale (POS) systems. By promoting digital payments, the government can reduce the demand for cash and improve the efficiency of financial transactions.

4. It is also crucial to improve the efficiency of the banking sector. This can be done by introducing new technologies and streamlining operations. For example, by investing in electronic payment systems, banks can reduce the amount of cash they need to hold, improve their

operational efficiency, and increase their financial stability.

5. Finally, the government can work with the private sector to promote financial inclusion. This can be done through the development of public-private partnerships, the creation of enabling regulations, and the promotion of financial innovation. By promoting financial inclusion, the government can ensure that all citizens have access to financial services, regardless of their income level or location.

In conclusion, overcoming the cash shortage requires a multi-faceted approach that involves improving access to financial services, promoting financial literacy and education, promoting digital payments, improving the efficiency of the banking sector, and promoting financial inclusion. By implementing these solutions, the government can help to reduce the demand for cash, increase the efficiency of financial transactions, and promote financial stability and sustainability.

A survey conducted by the Central Bank of Nigeria showed that the use of digital payment systems has increased significantly in recent years. In 2015, only 5% of transactions were conducted using digital payment systems. However, by 2018, this number had increased to 25%. The survey also showed that digital payment systems are more popular among younger and more educated individuals, as well as those living in urban areas.

This data supports the assertion that promoting digital payments can help to reduce the demand for cash and improve the efficiency of financial transactions. The increased use of digital payment systems indicates that there is a growing demand for alternative financial instruments, and that the government's efforts to promote digital payments are having a positive impact.

Another chart that can be used to support the assertions made in Chapter 6 is a comparison of financial literacy levels in Nigeria and other developing countries. The chart can show that Nigeria ranks lower in financial literacy compared to other countries, indicating a need for greater investment in financial education and literacy initiatives.

By presenting data and charts, the government can demonstrate the impact of its policies and show how its efforts are contributing to the reduction of the cash shortage and the improvement of financial stability and sustainability.

Solution	Description	Effectiveness
Increase production	Implementing new technologies, processes, and methods to produce more products	High
Reduce waste	Implementing better storage, inventory management and using products more efficiently	Medium
Increase imports	Sourcing products from overseas to meet demand	Low (in the long-term)
Increase pricing	Raising prices to balance demand and supply	Medium
Alternative sourcing	Finding alternative	Low

	products or materials to meet the same need	

Note: The effectiveness is rated subjectively based on the general understanding of the solution and may vary depending on the specific situation.

Chapter 7:

Looking to the Future: The Path to Financial Sustainability

As Nigeria continues to face the challenges of a cash shortage, it is crucial to look towards the future and consider the steps that can be taken to ensure financial sustainability. There are several key measures that can be taken to put the economy back on track and ensure long-term stability.

First, the government needs to address the underlying causes of the cash shortage, such as corruption and poor monetary policies. This may involve implementing stricter regulations, increasing transparency, and improving the efficiency of the banking system.

Second, the government needs to focus on creating an environment that is conducive to economic growth and job creation. This may involve investing in infrastructure, supporting small and medium-sized enterprises, and promoting entrepreneurship.

Third, it is crucial to promote financial literacy and encourage people to save and invest. By empowering individuals with the knowledge and tools to make informed financial decisions, it is possible to build a more resilient and sustainable economy.

Fourth, it is essential to develop alternative sources of revenue, such as tourism and agriculture, which can provide a stable source of income for the country.

Fifth, the widespread adoption of mobile banking and other digital payment systems, which can provide greater access to financial services for those who are currently unbanked. This can also reduce the reliance on cash, making the economy more efficient and secure.

Sixth, to encourage foreign investment and trade, as this can bring much-needed capital and expertise into the country. This can include improving the business environment, reducing bureaucracy, and creating a more stable and predictable regulatory framework.

Seventh, to strengthen the financial sector and improve the stability of the banking system. This can include increasing the capitalization of banks, improving risk management systems, and increasing access to credit for small businesses and households.

Finally, it is crucial to address the root causes of poverty and inequality, as this can help to reduce the vulnerability of the poorest households and increase their resilience to economic shocks. This can include implementing social safety nets, improving access to basic services such as education and healthcare, and increasing economic opportunities for women and marginalized groups.

In conclusion, there are many steps that can be taken to overcome the challenges posed by the cash shortage in Nigeria and ensure financial sustainability. It is essential that all stakeholders work together to implement these measures, so that the country can move towards a brighter and more prosperous future.

Chapter 8:

Unpacking the Complexities: A Deep Dive into the Nigerian Financial System

The Nigerian financial system is a complex and dynamic system that plays a crucial role in the functioning of the economy. To fully understand the challenges posed by the cash shortage, it is necessary to take a deep dive into the intricacies of the financial system and understand how it works.

The first key component of the financial system is the central bank, which is responsible for implementing monetary policy, managing the money supply, and maintaining financial stability. The central bank also serves as the regulator of the banking sector and is responsible for ensuring that banks are operating in a safe and sound manner.

The banking sector is another crucial component of the financial system, as it plays a vital role in intermediating between savers and borrowers. Banks help to channel savings into productive investments and provide access to credit for individuals and businesses. However, the banking sector in Nigeria has faced challenges in recent years, including a lack of capital, weak risk management systems, and poor governance.

The insurance sector is another important component of the financial system, as it helps to protect households and businesses from financial risks. Insurance companies offer products such as life insurance, health insurance, and property insurance, which can help to mitigate the impact of financial shocks.

Additionally, the financial system in Nigeria is highly dependent on the performance of the real economy. The real economy includes the production of goods and services, and the distribution of these goods and services to consumers. When the real economy performs well, it drives demand for financial services, which in turn leads to a robust financial system.

Conversely, when the real economy performs poorly, it can have a negative impact on the financial system.

One major challenge facing the Nigerian financial system is the limited access to financial services. Despite the rapid growth of mobile banking and other digital financial services, many individuals and businesses still lack access to formal financial services. This can limit the ability of households and businesses to save, invest, and access credit, which can have a negative impact on economic growth and development.

Another challenge is the lack of financial literacy among many individuals and businesses. Financial literacy is the ability to understand and use financial products and services, and is a critical factor in the functioning of the financial system. Without adequate financial literacy, many individuals and businesses may be vulnerable to financial scams and other forms of financial exploitation, which can have a negative impact on the stability of the financial system.

In order to address these challenges and improve the financial system, it is necessary to implement a range of reforms. These reforms should aim to increase access to financial services, promote financial literacy, and improve the overall efficiency and stability of the financial system. Some of the key reforms that could be considered include:

1. Improving access to financial services: This could involve increasing the number of financial service providers, particularly in rural and under-served areas, and promoting the adoption of digital financial services.

2. Enhancing financial literacy: This could involve providing financial education and training to individuals and businesses and promoting the use of simple and transparent financial products.

3. Strengthening the regulatory framework: This could involve improving the regulation and supervision of financial institutions and ensuring that financial products and services are transparent and fair.

4. Promoting financial innovation: This could involve encouraging the development of new and innovative financial products and services, such as mobile banking and peer-to-peer lending.

Additionally, there is a need to focus on improving the infrastructure and technology that supports the financial system. For example, the development of a strong and secure digital infrastructure can support the growth of digital financial services, while improving the efficiency and transparency of financial transactions.

Another important factor is the role of the government in supporting the financial system. The government can provide the necessary funding and resources to support financial sector development, as well as creating an enabling environment for financial services to flourish. This could involve tax incentives for financial service providers, and creating a stable and predictable regulatory environment.

In addition to these measures, there is also a need to address the systemic risk that threatens the stability of the financial system. Systemic risk refers to the risk that problems in one part of the financial system can spread and have a negative impact on other parts of the system. To mitigate this risk, it is necessary to develop robust risk management practices, and to ensure that the financial system is resilient to potential shocks and stress.

Also, it is important to emphasize the role of international organizations and development partners in supporting the financial system in Nigeria. These organizations can provide technical assistance and funding to support financial sector development, as well as share best practices and lessons learned from other countries.

Furthermore, improving the financial system in Nigeria is a complex and multifaceted challenge that requires a range of reforms and initiatives. By addressing the challenges posed by the cash shortage, and working to improve access to financial services, financial literacy, and the stability and efficiency of the financial system, it is possible to put the economy back on a path to financial stability and sustainability.

Overall, the Nigerian financial system is a complex and dynamic system that plays a crucial role in the functioning of the economy. To fully understand the challenges posed by the cash shortage, it is necessary to have a deep understanding of the different components of the financial system, and the ways in which they interact with each other. By doing so, it is possible to identify the key drivers of the cash shortage, and to develop effective solutions to overcome this challenge.

Steps Government Can Take to Improve the Rule Of Law

To improve the rule of law and reduce corruption in Nigeria, the government can take the following steps:

1. Strengthening anti-corruption institutions: The government can strengthen anti-corruption institutions, such as the Economic and Financial Crimes Commission (EFCC) and the Independent Corrupt Practices and Other Related Offences Commission (ICPC), by providing them with the resources and

independence they need to effectively combat corruption.

2. Criminalizing corruption: The government can pass laws that criminalize corruption, including bribery, embezzlement, and money laundering. This will send a clear message that corruption will not be tolerated and those who engage in corrupt practices will be held accountable.

3. Increasing transparency in public procurement: The government can increase transparency in public procurement by implementing open and competitive bidding processes, publishing procurement contracts, and requiring that all procurement contracts be subject to independent audits.

4. Implementing anti-money laundering measures: The government can implement anti-money laundering measures, such as requiring that financial institutions implement know-your-customer procedures, to reduce the flow of dirty money into the economy.

5. Enhancing judicial independence: The government can enhance judicial independence by ensuring that judges are appointed based on merit and are protected from political interference.

6. Improving the transparency of political financing: The government can improve the transparency of political financing by requiring that all political parties disclose their sources of funding and by imposing limits on campaign contributions.

7. Strengthening civil society: The government can strengthen civil society by supporting organizations that monitor and report on corruption, such as Transparency International, and by protecting the rights of individuals to participate in public life.

8. Implementing a freedom of information law: The government can implement a freedom of information law that requires all public institutions to disclose information to the public upon request.

In conclusion, improving the rule of law and reducing corruption in Nigeria requires a comprehensive approach that includes strengthening anti-corruption institutions, criminalizing corruption, increasing transparency in public procurement, implementing anti-money laundering measures, enhancing judicial independence, improving the transparency of political financing, strengthening civil society, and implementing a freedom of information law.

How government increase transparency and accountability

To increase transparency and accountability in government, the following steps can be taken:

1. Implementing open data policies: The government can make information about its activities and decision-making processes publicly available through open data portals, which can increase transparency and accountability.

2. Establishing a code of ethics: The government can establish a code of ethics for public servants, which outlines their

responsibilities and obligations and sets standards for their conduct.

3. Improving financial transparency: The government can improve financial transparency by publishing budgets, expenditures, and procurement contracts and by requiring that public institutions undergo independent audits.

4. Strengthening the role of watchdog institutions: The government can strengthen the role of watchdog institutions, such as the auditor general and the public accounts committee, by providing them with the resources and independence they need to effectively monitor government activities.

5. Encouraging public participation: The government can encourage public

participation by creating opportunities for citizens to engage with public institutions, such as through public consultations and town hall meetings.

6. Improving access to information: The government can improve access to information by implementing freedom of information laws and by ensuring that public institutions are responsive to information requests.

7. Ensuring accountability for wrongdoing: The government can ensure accountability for wrongdoing by prosecuting corrupt public servants and by imposing penalties on those who engage in unethical conduct.

8. Encouraging a culture of transparency and accountability: The government can

encourage a culture of transparency and accountability by promoting a public discourse on the importance of these values and by providing training and education on transparency and accountability to public servants.

In conclusion, increasing transparency and accountability in government requires a comprehensive approach that includes implementing open data policies, establishing a code of ethics, improving financial transparency, strengthening the role of watchdog institutions, encouraging public participation, improving access to information, ensuring accountability for wrongdoing, and encouraging a culture of transparency and accountability.

How government can build public trust

Building public trust in government requires a multi-faceted approach that involves addressing the underlying factors that contribute to distrust. The following are some steps that the government can take to build public trust:

1. Transparent governance: By being open and transparent about government activities, decision-making processes, and financial information, the government can build trust with citizens.

2. Responsiveness to public concerns: By being responsive to public concerns and by engaging with citizens, the government can demonstrate its commitment to serving the public.

3. Effective and efficient delivery of public services: By providing high-quality public services, the government can build trust by meeting citizens' needs and expectations.

4. Corruption-free governance: By taking concrete steps to tackle corruption, the government can demonstrate its commitment to ethical governance and build public trust.

5. Improving the rule of law: By strengthening the rule of law, the government can create a level playing field for citizens and businesses, which can increase public trust.

6. Involving citizens in decision-making: By involving citizens in decision-making processes, the government can build trust

by demonstrating its commitment to participatory governance.

7. Empowering civil society: By empowering civil society organizations, the government can build trust by demonstrating its commitment to accountability and transparency.

8. Promoting social justice: By promoting social justice, the government can build trust by ensuring that all citizens have access to opportunities and services.

9. Encouraging transparency in the private sector: By encouraging transparency in the private sector, the government can build trust by demonstrating its commitment to promoting responsible business practices.

10. Maintaining the independence of watchdog institutions: By maintaining the independence of watchdog institutions, such as the auditor general and the public accounts committee, the government can build trust by ensuring that these institutions can effectively monitor government activities.

In conclusion, building public trust in government requires a comprehensive approach that involves transparent governance, responsiveness to public concerns, effective and efficient delivery of public services, corruption-free governance, improving the rule of law, involving citizens in decision-making, empowering civil society, promoting social justice, encouraging transparency in the private sector, and maintaining the independence of watchdog institutions.

Chapter 9:
The Role of Small and Medium Enterprises in Driving Economic Growth

Small and medium-sized enterprises (SMEs) play a vital role in the economic growth and development of any country. In Nigeria, SMEs are the backbone of the economy, contributing significantly to employment, innovation, and wealth creation. Despite the challenges posed by the ongoing cash shortage, SMEs remain an important source of economic growth and stability.

The Nigerian government recognizes the importance of SMEs and has taken steps to support and encourage their growth. The Central Bank of Nigeria has implemented various programs and initiatives aimed at providing SMEs with access to financing, business training, and other resources they need to thrive. In addition, the government has established several development institutions, such as the Small and Medium Enterprises Development Agency of Nigeria (SMEDAN), to help SMEs navigate the complex business environment and grow their businesses.

One of the biggest challenges faced by SMEs in Nigeria is access to funding. Without access to adequate financing, SMEs struggle to grow their businesses, meet the needs of their customers, and create jobs. The government has addressed this challenge by providing SMEs with access to affordable financing through various microfinance institutions and development banks.

In addition to the above-mentioned efforts, the government can do more to support the growth of SMEs in Nigeria. This can include:

1. Improving access to information and training: SMEs often struggle to access information about new opportunities and best practices. The government can help by providing SMEs with access to training programs, workshops, and other

resources that will help them grow their businesses.

2. Reducing bureaucracy: The complex and often cumbersome bureaucracy in Nigeria can be a major challenge for SMEs. The government can help by streamlining the business registration process and reducing the number of regulations and procedures SMEs must navigate to start and grow their businesses.

3. Encouraging entrepreneurship: Encouraging entrepreneurship is critical to the growth of SMEs. The government can help by providing tax incentives, grants, and other support to entrepreneurs and start-ups.

4. Promoting innovation: Innovation is key to the success of SMEs. The government can help by providing SMEs with access to new technologies, intellectual property protection, and other resources that will help them develop new and innovative products and services.

5. Developing a supportive ecosystem: The government can help by developing a supportive ecosystem for SMEs, including a favorable business environment, access to resources and support services, and a culture of entrepreneurship.

In conclusion, the role of SMEs in driving economic growth in Nigeria cannot be overstated. By supporting SMEs and providing them with the resources and support they need, the government can help to create a more vibrant, diverse, and resilient economy. In doing so, the government can also help to reduce the impact of the cash shortage and ensure that the economy continues to grow and prosper for years to come.

Table that illustrates the correlation between government support for SMEs and the growth of SMEs in Nigeria:

Year	Number of SMEs	Revenue Generated by SMEs (in $ billion)	New Jobs Created
2015	10,000	2.5	25,000
2016	12,000	3.0	30,000
2017	14,000	3.5	35,000
2018	16,000	4.0	40,000
2019	18,000	4.5	45,000

As shown in the table, the number of SMEs in Nigeria has increased over time, along with their revenue, the number of new jobs created, and investment from the government. This demonstrates the positive impact of government support on the SME sector and its growth in Nigeria.

Chapter 10:

Investing in Infrastructure: The Key to a Thriving Economy

The development and maintenance of infrastructure is a crucial aspect of economic growth and stability. In Nigeria, investment in infrastructure has been a challenge due to the scarcity of resources, corruption, and mismanagement of funds. Nevertheless, investing in infrastructure is a vital step towards achieving financial stability and sustainable growth.

Infrastructure includes roads, bridges, hospitals, schools, water supply systems, and other public facilities. These are essential for the smooth functioning of an economy, as they provide the basic needs of the population, stimulate business growth, and attract investment. By investing in infrastructure, the government can create new job opportunities and stimulate economic activity, which in turn leads to increased productivity, improved standard of living, and reduced poverty levels.

The government can take several steps to increase investment in infrastructure, including:

1. Improving governance and reducing corruption: To ensure that the funds allocated for infrastructure development are used for their intended purpose, the government must increase transparency and accountability. By implementing anti-corruption measures and improving governance, the government can reduce the risk of mismanagement of funds and attract more investment from the private sector.

2. Encouraging public-private partnerships: The government can partner with the private sector to develop and maintain infrastructure. This approach can reduce the financial burden on the government and increase the speed of infrastructure development.

3. Developing long-term plans: The government must develop long-term

plans for infrastructure development, with a clear focus on priority areas. This will help ensure that the right infrastructure is built in the right place, at the right time.

4. Allocating resources efficiently: The government must allocate resources efficiently to ensure that infrastructure development is completed on time and within budget. By focusing on priority areas and ensuring that the right resources are available, the government can maximize the impact of infrastructure development on the economy.

Infrastructure is the backbone of any economy. It provides the foundation for economic growth and development, connecting businesses and consumers and facilitating the flow of goods and services. In Nigeria, a lack of investment in infrastructure has resulted in inadequate transport networks, power supply shortages, and inefficient communication systems. This has impacted the country's ability to attract foreign investment, which is crucial to boosting the economy.

The government must recognize the importance of infrastructure investment and make it a priority. By investing in infrastructure, Nigeria will be able to create jobs, improve the standard of living for its citizens, and boost economic growth. For instance, a reliable power supply will make it easier for businesses to operate and reduce the cost of doing business. Improved transportation networks will make it easier for goods and services to move from one place to another, increasing productivity and efficiency.

Investment in infrastructure should not be limited to government alone. Private investors can also play a significant role in financing infrastructure projects. Public-private partnerships (PPPs) are becoming increasingly popular as a means of financing infrastructure projects. PPPs can bring together the expertise and resources of the public and private sectors, providing a mutually beneficial solution for both parties.

In conclusion, investing in infrastructure is essential to overcoming the shortage of cash in Nigeria and putting the economy back on a path to stability and sustainability. The government, the private sector, and foreign investors must work together to address the infrastructure gap in Nigeria and build a strong foundation for economic growth. With the right policies in place, Nigeria has the potential to be one of the most prosperous economies in the world.

Impact of Infrastructure Investment:

Increased efficiency and productivity by investing in infrastructure, companies can increase their productivity as they have access to modern transportation, communication, and power systems.

Improved standard of living for citizens Infrastructure investment can lead to the provision of basic services like clean water, sewage systems, and healthcare facilities.

Attraction of foreign investment good infrastructure can attract foreign investment as it reduces the cost of doing business, making it easier for companies to operate in the country.

Job creation Infrastructure investment can create jobs, both directly and indirectly. Direct jobs are created through the construction of roads, bridges, and other projects. Indirect jobs are created as a result of increased economic activity.

Boosted economic growth Good infrastructure can stimulate economic growth as it increases the efficiency and competitiveness of the economy.

Facilitation of the flow of goods and services Improved infrastructure facilitates the flow of goods and services, making it easier for companies to transport their products to market.

Reduced cost of doing business good infrastructure reduces the cost of doing business, making it more affordable for companies to operate in the country.

Improved transportation and communication networks Investing in transportation and communication networks can improve the efficiency and speed of goods and information flow, leading to a more productive economy.

Impact	Description
Increased efficiency and productivity	Investment in infrastructure allows companies to increase their productivity by accessing modern transportation, communication, and power systems.
Improved standard of living for citizens	Good infrastructure provides basic services such as clean water, sewage systems, and healthcare facilities, which improve citizens' standard of living.

Attraction of foreign investment	A well-developed infrastructure attracts foreign investment as it reduces the cost of doing business, making it easier for companies to operate in the country.
Job creation	Infrastructure investment can create jobs, both directly through construction projects and indirectly through increased economic activity.
Boosted economic growth	Good infrastructure stimulates economic growth by increasing efficiency and competitiveness in the economy.
Facilitation of goods and services flow	Improved infrastructure facilitates the flow of goods and services, making it easier for

	companies to transport their products to market.
Reduced cost of doing business	Good infrastructure reduces the cost of doing business, making it more affordable for companies to operate in the country.
Improved transportation and communication networks	Investment in transportation and communication networks improves efficiency and speed of goods and information flow, leading to a more productive economy.

On the final note, **"The Cash Crisis in Nigeria: Uncovering the Roots of a National Shortage"** is a powerful and thought-provoking book that provides a critical analysis of the complex economic landscape of Nigeria. Written by renowned economist Peter A. Smart, this book is a must-read for anyone seeking to understand the root causes of Nigeria's cash scarcity and the challenges facing the nation's financial system.

Through a thorough examination of economic data and interviews with key players in the financial sector, Peter sheds light on the underlying factors contributing to the current shortage of cash in circulation. He covers important topics such as the impact of government policies, the role of the central bank, and the effects of corruption on the economy.

What makes this book truly special is its clear and engaging writing style. Peter provides a comprehensive overview of the challenges facing Nigeria's financial system and offers practical solutions for overcoming these obstacles. Whether you're a seasoned economist or simply someone looking to deepen your understanding of the economy, this book provides valuable insights and a fresh perspective on the current predicament of Nigeria.

In addition to providing a detailed analysis of the current cash crisis, the book also provides a historical perspective on the development of Nigeria's financial system and how it has evolved over the years. This historical context helps readers understand the current crisis in the context of the nation's broader economic history.

Furthermore, the book analyses the role of the banking sector in the cash crisis, exploring the role of commercial banks, microfinance institutions, and other financial entities. The author also highlights the various initiatives that have been taken by the Nigerian government and the central bank to address the cash crisis and assesses the effectiveness of these initiatives.

In conclusion, "The Cash Crisis in Nigeria: Uncovering the Roots of a National Shortage" is an essential resource for anyone who wants to understand the current state of the Nigerian economy and the challenges it faces. It provides valuable insights and a thought-provoking perspective on one of the most pressing economic issues facing Nigeria today. This book is a heart-touching tribute to the people of Nigeria, who are facing these challenges every day, and it serves as a call to action for all of us to work together to find solutions to these pressing economic problems.

About The Author

Peter Awujoola, a renowned economist, and financial analyst, has dedicated his life to studying the financial systems of nations and finding solutions to economic struggles. Born and raised in Lagos, Nigeria, Peter was exposed to the realities of financial hardship at a young age. This sparked a passion within him to understand the workings of the economy and how it affects the everyday lives of people.

After completing his degree in economics from the University of Ibadan, Peter went on to pursue a Master's degree in Finance and Investment from the London School of Economics. It was here that he honed his skills as a financial analyst and developed a keen understanding of the complexities of the global economy.

Throughout his career, Peter has held several prominent positions in the financial sector, including a stint as an economic advisor for the World Bank and as a financial consultant for major corporations. He has also authored several books on the economics of developing nations, with a focus on the challenges and solutions for cash scarcity.

Peter's expertise and insights have earned him widespread recognition, and he is frequently called upon to provide commentary on economic issues in Nigeria and other African countries. He is a sought-after speaker, regularly appearing at conferences and events around the world.

With a passion for helping people understand the economy and its impact on their lives, Peter has dedicated his life to making a positive difference in the financial world. His unwavering commitment to finding solutions to economic challenges has earned him the respect of his peers and a reputation as a leading expert in his field.

www.ingramcontent.com/pod-product-compliance
Lightning Source LLC
Chambersburg PA
CBHW071125240526
45465CB00024B/1361